Matchstick Mini is having a new baby brother or sister
By Edel Malone

Original concept created, illustrated, and written by Edel Malone. I'm sure you will love these books as much as I do. I know you will enjoy making lasting memories with your child moving forward in all stages of their lives by encouraging your child to tell you what's on their mind throughout their lifetime. Asking questions is the way forward. Check out the other Matchstick Mini books from this series.

I dedicate these books to all my nieces and nephews. "Matchstick Mini is having a new baby brother or sister"', all rights reserved to Edel Malone, no parts of this book can be used without permission ©copyright 2022 Thank you for buying my book. First edition 2022. For more information contact lifestylethoughtscoaching@gmail.com

The Matchstick Mini book series has been designed to encourage your child to open up and talk about what is on their mind from an early age. The topics covered are related to young children to encourage good communication techniques carrying on into each stage of their lives, keeping safety and values in mind. Sizes and colors may vary for printed books.

OTHER BOOKS FROM MATCHSTICK MINI

Matchstick Mini and safety

Matchstick Mini and others

Matchstick Mini has fun

Matchstick Mini and school

Matchstick Mini is very good

Matchstick Mini is healthy

Matchstick Mini is looking forward to having a new baby brother or sister, he is also worried about having a baby brother or sister, and that's okay too. Matchstick Mini knows it is okay to feel excited and nervous because he doesn't know what it would be like to have a baby brother or sister. Matchstick Mini wonders will he get less attention when the baby comes, and he shouldn't be worried because there is enough love to go around for everyone.

Matchstick Mini likes to play on his own, he loves to use his imagination, and he loves to play all different kinds of games with his toys. He even likes to practice some of his sports on his own too. For example, he practices his football, basketball, boxing, and gymnastic skills and always has lots of fun on his own when there is no one else around to play with.

Even though Matchstick Mini likes to play on his own and he loves his alone time, he loves when his friends or cousins come over to play in his house and he loves going to visit their houses too. Matchstick Mini knows some games are more fun when you have more people, especially sports, water fights, tea parties, and it would be nice to have other people to talk to. Matchstick Mini and his friends have fun building forts and playing in the garden too.

Matchstick Mini starts to think it could be nice to have a baby brother or sister to play games with, build Lego, make forts, and have tea parties, and he thinks it would be nice to have a little brother or sister to talk to too. Matchstick Mini wonders if they would like the same toys and would like to do the same things. Matchstick Mini wonders if his new baby brother or sister would like superhero toys, princess toys, building toys, or different toys to the ones he likes.

Matchstick Mini knows that brothers and sisters come in all different kinds of ways. Some people have a mammy and a daddy, and some have step mammies and step daddies too. Some children have stepsisters and brothers from other families, some have two mammies or two daddies, some have one parent, and some have guardians. Matchstick Mini thinks families being different is cool.

Some people have their babies born at home instead of at a hospital, and other people have babies in the hospital. Some of Matchstick Mini's friends have brothers and sisters that don't live with them. Matchstick Mini's new baby brother or sister will stay in his house all the time once the new baby is born. Matchstick Mini loves that everyone is different.

HOSPITAL

Matchstick Mini starts to believe that there is enough love to go around for everyone, he knows everyone loves to spend time with each other, and not everyone can spend the same amount of time together. Some families live in separate houses sometimes, and adults must go to work, and children must go to school. Everyone can go on days out together and sometimes some people from the same family don't go because they are busy minding the baby or must stay at home and look after grandparents or mind people who are sick. Do you believe there is enough love to go around for everyone?

Matchstick Mini likes to have company, and he loves to ask questions and some games are more fun with others. Even though Matchstick Mini likes to be on his own, he has fun with everyone too. Matchstick Mini loves talking to his family and friends and loves asking them if they have any news.

Matchstick Mini likes to share his toys with his friends when they come over, and Matchstick Mini thinks it would be nice to have a little brother or sister to share toys with too. Do you like to share with your family and friends like Matchstick Mini?

Matchstick Mini knows that everyone is of different ages and at different ages, people do different things, and he knows babies don't walk or talk until they are older. He knows it would be fun to see a baby brother or sister learning how to crawl and walk, and Matchstick Mini thinks when the baby gets older, he could help teach them how to play games and have lots of fun.

Matchstick Mini knows that everyone lives different lives, some people live in apartments or houses or other places, and everyone has different families. Some people have loads of people in their family, and some people have smaller families. He knows each person in all families does other things every day. He loves that some people go to work, some children go to playschool, older children go to big school, and babies sleep most of the day and drink bottles and poop.

Matchstick Mini understands that babies need a lot of attention until they start walking, talking, and using the toilet instead of nappies. Matchstick Mini knows babies are too small to do these things by themselves, so Matchstick Mini decides he won't be jealous when the baby needs a bit more time like he did when he was a baby, and he won't mind sharing his family time because there is enough love for everyone. Everyone can be happy, and Matchstick Mini wants to enjoy his little brother or sister growing up.

I won't
be
jealous

Matchstick Mini looks forward to teaching his little brother or sister how to collect leaves on days out to draw when they get home. Even though he knows it will take time and he will have to wait on the baby to get older. Matchstick Mini decides to get excited about having a new baby brother or sister, and he doesn't worry anymore. He looks forward to them growing up together. Matchstick Mini thinks having a new baby brother or sister is something to look forward to.

Matchstick Mini knows that when the baby comes, the house will be a bit different because there will be new toys, and the baby might cry when the baby is tired or hungry, he knows a baby crying is the baby's way of telling everyone they are tired or hungry because they aren't able to talk. Matchstick Mini won't get nervous when the baby is crying because it is normal to hear babies crying. Matchstick Mini will tell the baby it's okay when they are crying, and if an adult doesn't know the baby is crying, he will tell an adult. Matchstick Mini thinks having a new baby brother or sister will be cool.

it's
OKAY

Printed in Great Britain
by Amazon